ID618461

FOURTH STEPS IN BALLET: ON YOUR TOES!

Fourth Steps in Ballet: On Your Toes!

BASIC POINTE WORK

Thalia Mara

ILLUSTRATED BY LOUISE HOLMGREN

A DANCE HORIZONS BOOK
Princeton Book Company, Publishers
Princeton, New Jersey

Reprinted 1987 Princeton Book Company, Publishers
P.O. Box 109
Princeton, NJ 08542

This is an unabridged republication of the first edition published
in 1959 by Garden City Books, Garden City, N.Y.

ISBN 916622-56-8

Library of Congress Catalog Card Number 74-181476

Printed in the United States of America

FOREWORD

The dance on pointe, or "toe dancing" as it is popularly called, is part of the art of academic classical ballet.

It is the ultimate in technical attainment for the female ballet dancer.

Although the art of ballet is some three hundred years old, dancing on the tips of the toes did not come into being until the early part of the nineteenth century. It is believed that it was invented by Philippe Taglioni for his daughter Marie, who was one of the greatest ballerinas of her day.

The purpose of rising to the ends of the toes was to give a quality of lightness and ethereality to the dance. The romantic ballet was born in the 1830's, and this use of the pointes in dancing helped to convey a feeling of supernatural lightness and an "out of this world" quality to the dancers who were portraying wraiths, sylphs, and vilis in such ballets as *La Sylphide* and *Giselle*.

The early dancers such as Marie Taglioni, Fanny Cerrito, Lucille Grahn, and Carlotta Grisi, all of whom were famed exponents of the romantic ballet, wore unblocked slippers —that is, their slippers were not stiffened at the toes— but achieved some measure of support by darning the ends of the slippers. They did not, of course, perform the very difficult technical feats that ballerinas today are called upon to perform but were content with a few simple *relevés* and *piqués*.

The acrobatic qualities of "toe dancing" seem to have caught the fancies of the music-hall public early in the twentieth century, and this phase of ballet technique soon degenerated into vulgar displays of acrobatic tricks even up to the point of "tap on toe" and vaudeville acts in which girls jumped rope and up and down flights of stairs "on toe."

For some inexplicable reason children are fascinated by "toe dancing," believing it to be the epitome of glamor, and every little girl who studies dance dreams of dancing on her toes.

Actually, the only children who should dance on their pointes are those who are training for a professional career in ballet, for the training is rigorous and requires several years of intensive technical training to develop the muscular strength of the back, the thighs, and the insteps prior to this difficult and advanced stage of development. Most children who do not plan to enter the profession do not have the time or the inclination to devote the hours of dedicated work required.

However, since I am aware that thousands of youngsters will continue to demand "toe shoes" from their ballet teachers, in spite of whatever I may say, it is my purpose in this book to set forth, as clearly as possible, the correct aspects of the technical training in the hope that it will help to clear up some popular misconceptions and to correct some evils that exist through bad and careless teaching.

It is with joy that I have seen the art of ballet grow in popular appeal in the U. S., during the past twenty years, from a "high-brow art" appreciated by only a few to the place it now holds in the public esteem. Yet there are many dangers inherent in this newly found popularity.

Parents, seeing the beautiful ballerinas on the stage, screen, and television, are convinced that a year or two of study will give their daughters the beautiful posture, the poise, and the grace of these dancers. And so hundreds of thousands of children are enrolled annually in the dancing schools. This would be wonderful if there were enough good teachers to meet this popular demand or if people were so informed concerning ballet that they would demand the proper kind of training. Unfortunately this is not the case. There are many teachers who profess to teach ballet but who do not possess the necessary background of training themselves to undertake safely the training of others, particularly young children. And, unhappily, the general public is still uninformed about the true facts of ballet. The combination of these circumstances leads to a great deal of abuse in the name of ballet and to actual physical damage to many children.

One of the greatest evils committed by poor teachers is the "toe dancing" lessons which they give to physically unprepared children and children who are entirely too young to learn this form of dancing with safety.

Doctors will tell you that the bones of the toes are the last bones of the foot to be developed and that up to the age of sixteen years these bones, and many others of the foot, are really cartilage similar to that of the nose or the ear. It is not until after the tenth year that these soft and malleable bones begin to harden, prior to this time the feet cannot take the strain and stress of toe dancing without injury or even deformity.

A well-trained ballet teacher understands this because a knowledge of anatomy is a prerequisite for anyone who deals with the physical development of the body. In professional schools that train children for the ballet stage the children are carefully watched and nurtured in the development of their training. Training in academic technique does not begin before the age of eight, and several years are spent subsequently in technical exercises that develop the needed strength and muscle tone.

Ballet exercises are soundly scientific. When correctly administered they build a beautiful, sound, symmetrical body. Since the feet are so important in ballet dancing its exercises are so planned that they remake the feet into instruments of dance—they become strong, extremely supple, and sensitive. Under the proper teaching and careful supervision of a good teacher toe dancing will not be harmful. But in the hands of a poor teacher these same exercises can injure the child's feet, knees, and back.

There are no hard and fast rules as to when a child should begin the study of pointe work. Each child is an individual case. No child should begin before the age of ten, nor without several years of training in soft slippers. This training should not consist of learning only "routines" but should be training in academic exercises.

The teacher, alone, should determine when the child is ready to begin this phase of training—this decision will be based on the child's response to the training, on her weight, strength, ability, and muscle tone. As can be readily seen, this will vary with each student.

In *First Steps in Ballet* I have dealt with the basic exercises at the barre that build the strength of the dancer, and I have discussed in detail the correct "placement" of the body. It is this "placement" that determines the readiness of the student. Preliminary training in ballet is concerned primarily with posture—the effort is to develop the strength of the postural muscles of the back, for it is these muscles that give control of the body to the dancer. No student should attempt pointe work until perfect posture is part of her being. When the dancer can stand straight, with the head in proper alignment to the spine, and rise to the *demi-pointe* (the balls of the feet) maintaining this perfect alignment as well as tightly pulled-up knees and the weight of the body lifted from the feet, pulled up and distributed through the body, she is ready to begin the study of pointe work.

Dancing on the pointes is a serious affair and should not be undertaken lightly. It is my earnest hope that every parent of every child who studies ballet will, someday, realize that the toe slippers should not be given as Christmas presents to a child who is not prepared to use them properly, that the teacher is not just being a "meanie" who needs to be cajoled into letting Susie (who is just dying to get up on her toes) have her way because her friend "Joanie, who studies in that other dancing school, got her toe shoes right away."

Deformed toes, painful bunion joints, and nagging backaches are the result of wrong training at too early an age. Once the damage is done, it cannot be undone. Use caution then—forewarned is forearmed!

Thalia Mara

CONTENTS

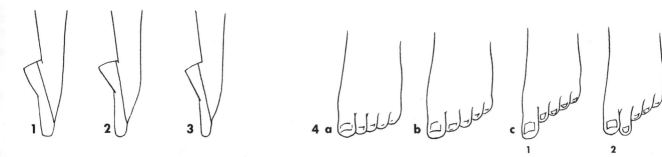

THE FOOT

1. The ideal foot for dancing *sur les pointes* is the square foot—one that gives the impression that the toes are sawed off straight across—with a low arch and a solid, strong ankle. Such a foot will "wear well" and will be a great comfort to the dancer because in standing on pointe the weight of the body will be borne evenly by all of the toes.

2. This foot, while more beautiful in appearance because of its high arch (beginning almost in the ankle) and its slim, well-turned ankle, is much more difficult to work with because of its great flexibility and softness. Even with excellent training and care it will never be so strong as the foot illustrated in Figure 1. Dancers with this type of foot must be especially careful in their training and must go through a longer preparatory period before attempting to dance on pointes.

3. Another type of high arch; this one, however, is stronger than the foot illustrated in Figure 2 because the arch does not involve the ankle joint.

4. The grouping of the toes is very important to the would-be ballet dancer: a. short toes, all even in length, are the best for pointe work because all of the toes will share the burden of the dancer's weight; b. at least three toes should be "carriers"; c. 1 and 2. when one toe is longer than the rest, the dancer finds toe work difficult and painful.

11

THE CARE OF THE FEET

With a reasonable amount of care your feet will be none the worse for dancing on the tips of your toes *provided that you are properly prepared physically* when you begin this phase of balletic technique.

The skin of the toes and the entire foot should be kept dry, soft, and pliant at all times. It should not be allowed to dry out so that it cracks, or to become moist and tender so that it rubs off, blisters, or forms soft corns between the toes.

A good practice to follow is a nightly massage with a bit of Vaseline after the feet are bathed and thoroughly dried. Be sure to dry well between the toes, then rub a tiny amount of Vaseline into the skin of the toes, working it in until it disappears. Push a little into the space around the toenails with an orangewood stick to prevent the formation of calluses between the nail and the skin, particularly in the big toes. Pay special attention to the skin on the heels at the back so that it does not become dry and cracked. During the massage take hold of each toe individually, pull it and stretch it a little, and move it around. Knead the metatarsal arch with the thumb, particularly around the big-toe joint. Wipe off any excess Vaseline; do not leave the feet greasy. Consistent daily care of this sort will pay off in skin that is soft and pliant and that does not rub off easily or blister or crack.

Inevitably, if you dance long enough and advance to the point where you do many difficult things and where you spend many hours dancing on pointe, you will have occasion to deal with blisters and rubbed toes. One way to deal with this condition is to use "New Skin," a commercial preparation that can be bought in the drugstore and that puts a protective coating over the raw spot until the skin can grow over it again. Follow the directions on the package if you use this preparation. Another way to cope with a blister or rubbed toe is to put a dab of boric-acid ointment on the raw spot, after using a little Mercurochrome or iodine on it, then cover it well with a waterproof adhesive bandage. Change the dressing daily and do not allow the affected toe to get wet.

The toenails must be kept short for toe dancing. Long toenails will bruise and cause the feet to feel very sore. If there is a tendency toward ingrown toenails, cut the nail a little shorter in the center like the letter U. Students are sometimes alarmed when they develop a toenail that thickens and grows off, but this need not bother anyone. It is usually the result of a bruise or of pressure on that particular toe. A nail that grows off is always replaced by a new one growing underneath the old one.

If there is a good podiatrist—chiropodist in your area, it is a good idea to visit him periodically and let him check over your feet and nails.

For those students who have one toe longer than the

others there will always be a problem. If the condition is not too marked, the dancer can sometimes learn to work with it. In this case it is helpful to wrap the longer toe in a little lamb's wool or tissue paper under the stocking. If, however, the one toe is much longer than any of the others, the student will find it impossible to dance on pointe because the condition will always cause a great deal of pain.

THE SLIPPERS

In order to dance well the dancer must wear the correct kind of slippers, and these must be properly fitted to the feet.

Unfortunately there is a very wide popular misconception concerning "toe shoes"—their construction, their fitting, and their care.

The properly made slipper must be hand-sewn, very lightly "boxed" or "blocked" (the hard portion at the end of the slipper), and must be completely flexible and light in weight. The slipper should fit the foot like a glove so that it does not impede the dancer's movements.

The current use of stiff, hard, heavy shoes stems from the fact that there is so much poor and careless teaching of ballet. A student who has been improperly prepared for pointe work lacks muscle tone and the necessary strength in the feet, thighs, and back to support herself

in standing on the tip ends of the toes. Therefore the necessity for a shoe that is constructed so strongly that it will support the wearer's entire weight. In other words, since the dancer lacks the trained strength to support herself, the manufacturers of ballet slippers have endeavored to help her by producing shoes that will do the work she should be doing herself.

The drawback here is that shoes of this weight and stiffness make it impossible for the dancer to use her feet properly.

At all times the dancer must have control of her feet for balance, and the ability to move freely and with ease depends on this. This is just as true when wearing toe slippers as when wearing soft ballet slippers. The dancer must be able to "feel" the floor with her toes, must be able to use the *demi-pointe* level of the foot as freely as the full-pointe level. Without this ability to use the *demi-pointe* the dancer's movements must, of necessity, be jerky and hard because she will have to jump off her toes instead of rolling down smoothly.

From the very beginning the dancer must be trained on the correct slippers. Once dependence on the hard, stiff shoes has been established it is very difficult, sometimes impossible, to make the change to the correct, light slippers because it means learning a completely new way to dance on the pointes.

The right type of slipper may not be easy to find, particularly for those living in a small community. However, they are worth searching for and your dancing teacher can order them for you directly from the manufacturers.

The proper fitting of the slippers is vitally important too. Toe slippers *must* fit the feet snugly. They should not be bought "large enough to grow into," they must be bought for the present time. This is absolutely necessary for two reasons—the protection of the feet and the aesthetic appearance. Slippers that are too large may easily cause the wearer to fall or to sprain the ankle or forefoot because there can be no balance in slippers that are too large. They will look ugly because they will not conform to the dancer's foot as she points. Actually, the slipper should fit the foot like a glove so that it bends and shapes with the movements of the foot.

Like all ballet slippers the toe slippers are fitted shorter than street shoes. This may be anywhere from one to two sizes shorter and one width wider than street shoes. In trying on the slippers one should stand first on the whole foot (both feet). The ends of the toes should touch the end wall of the slipper with the toes stretched out straight. If the toes are pushed back, so that they are forced to curl up slightly, the slippers are too short. One should have to tug a little to get the slippers on, they should not slip on and off like bedroom slippers. The width must be watched carefully, for the dancer must have freedom to move the foot—it must not be held as though in a vise.

When standing on pointe there should be no gap a the sides of the slippers—such a gap means that th slipper is too large.

The length of the slipper's vamp must be determine by the length of the dancer's toes. A long-toed foot re quires a longer vamp than a short-toed foot. This is mos important, for a difference as little as one eighth of a inch in the length of the vamp can alter the dancer' position on pointe. If the vamp is too short, it will caus the foot to break over at the toes, making it look extremel ugly. If, on the other hand, the vamp is too long, it wi throw the dancer back and prevent her from attaining full-pointe position.

The only thing that should be used inside the slipper to protect the toes is a little lamb's wool—*very little!* Th sole purpose of using this wool is to protect the skin o the toes from rubbing. Later, as the skin toughens up the use of the wool can be entirely discontinued.

There is a horrible practice among some students i this country—the use of "bunny pads" made of fur or even worse, sponge-rubber pads. Nothing could be wors for the feet, to say nothing of the fact that it is impos sible to dance well when wearing such contraption First, the slippers will have to be worn several sizes to large in order to accommodate the pads. Second, the fu and the rubber both make the feet perspire profusel his makes the skin tender, causes it to crack and rub off, and makes soft corns and blisters. The feet must be kept as dry as possible for good health reasons as well as good dancing reasons. Third, the wearer of these pads has absolutely no contact with the floor, therefore no sure footing and no balance.

One should never be afraid to dance in soft slippers. When the boxing at the toes softens up sufficiently to permit the dancer to feel the floor, the dancer is able to do her best work. This is what is meant by "breaking in" a pair of toe slippers. When putting on a pair of new slippers, for the first time, it will help to soften them up so that they conform and mold to the movements of the feet more easily. This may be done by taking each shoe individually, grasping it firmly in one hand, and kneading gently with the heel of the other hand all over the boxed portion.

No toe slipper will last forever. Naturally, the more advanced the dancer and the more work done in the slippers, the quicker they will wear out. Since this can become an expensive factor in your dance studies, here are some tips from Mr. James Selva for preserving the life of your slippers.

Keep two pairs in use at the same time, using them alternately in order to permit each pair to dry out thoroughly between uses.

Never wet the backs of the heels of the slippers with water, as so many students do in order to keep the slipper from slipping off at the heel. The water opens the pores of the leather, robbing it of its life and resiliency. Also, since the boxing at the toe end is made by layers of glue, the water will destroy the glue and cause the slipper to lose its shape and every vestige of support. (A dab of glue on the heel of your stocking or an elastic loop such as illustrated in Figure 9 will keep your slipper on better.)

After using the slippers fold them up neatly, wrap them in a clean towel, and keep them in a dry place in your practice bag, separate from your damp practice clothes. As soon as possible take them out of the practice bag and open them up, allowing them to air thoroughly until the next time they are used.

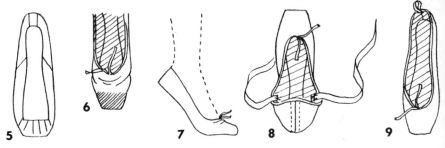

5

6

7

8

9

SELECTING AND PREPARING THE SLIPPERS

In selecting your slippers look for the following:

5. The satin of the toe slipper must be gathered into pleats on the underside of the slipper just as it is in soft ballet slippers. These pleats are absolutely essential, for they provide for the expansion and movement of the toes. Incidentally, the presence of these pleats is your proof that the slipper is hand-constructed.

6. The boxing should be light.

7. The sole of the slipper must be flexible to permit the use of the *demi-pointe*. If the sole is very thick at the toe end and too stiff to permit the shoe to bend in this fashion, it is not the proper kind of slipper, for it will not permit the correct use of the feet.

In preparing the slippers for use note these suggestions:

8. To find the correct place on which to sew the ribbons, bend the back of the slipper down until it touches the inner sole. Sew the end of the ribbon at the fold, attaching it to the canvas inner lining about midway between the binding and the sole. Do not stitch through the satin and do not sew to the binding, for the drawstring must remain free. The ribbon should be about three quarters of an inch in width and made of heavy satin. To prevent the knot from slipping and untying, and the ribbon from rolling up like a string, line the inside of the ribbon with cotton tape, sewing it to the ribbon with tiny stitches. About one inch of the end of the ribbon should be folded under before it is sewn to the shoe in order to make the attachment strong and eliminate any raveling. Sew the ribbon on with heavy thread, using cross-stitches. Clip the ends of the ribbon on the bias to prevent fraying.

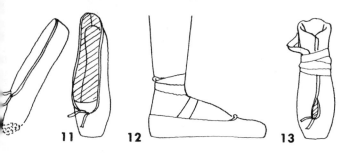

11   **12**   **13**

9. An elastic loop sewn to the inside back of the heel will help to keep the slippers on at the heels if one has trouble with this.

10. Darning helps to preserve the slipper for longer use because it prevents the satin from fraying. Use an embroidery needle and embroidery cotton of the same color as the slipper. You will also need a thimble and a little pair of pliers as it is difficult to pull the needle through the stiff material of the boxed toe. The darning covers the entire toe of the slipper at the bottom and the tip of the end. It should not extend over the top of the toe. After the darning is completed, cover it with a thin layer of colorless shellac and hang the slippers up to dry, allowing several days for the shellac to dry thoroughly.

11. If you find that the vamp is too short and that you break across the toes as you stand on pointe, sew a piece of strong heavy ribbon (not elastic) across the top of the vamp at the inside.

12. A properly tied shoe. The ribbons must always be straight (and clean!), not rolled up into strings. Tie a secure knot and tuck the ends of the ribbons out of sight. Draw the drawstrings, tie them securely (a bow is best so that they can be readjusted easily), and tuck them inside under the vamp.

13. Put your shoes away carefully if you want them to last. Fold the back in to the inner sole, fold both sides over, wrap the ribbons around and tuck the ends in.

14. DON'T DO THIS!

14

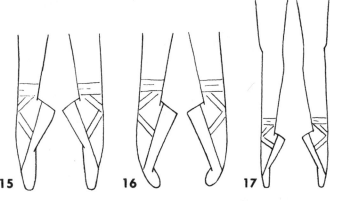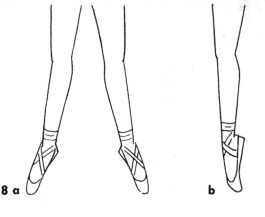

15   **16**   **17**   **18 a**   **b**

POSITION ON POINTE

CORRECT POSITION

15. In standing correctly on the pointes the dancer stands on the pads of the toes pulling the weight upward from them as much as possible.

INCORRECT POSITION

16. Never push down on the toes, curling them over so that you stand on the knuckles.

CORRECT POSITION

17. The foot must be in its proper alignment when standing on pointe. Toes must be aligned to heel and foot must be aligned to leg.

INCORRECT POSITION

18. a. Sickle in

       b. Sickle out

The arch must be developed through strength, not weakness. To achieve this strength, the dancer must be constantly pulling up through the insteps, not pushing down when standing on pointes. Do not press down on the feet so that they bear the weight of the body and you dance on your knuckles, as in Figure 16, but pull the weight of the body upward to take as much of it as possible off the toes. This develops the insteps correctly, giving them strength and stability.

RELEVÉS

There are two correct ways to relevé—that is, to rise from the whole foot, with the heel firmly planted on the floor, to the full-pointe position. One is to roll up through the instep, keeping the toes in their original place and lifting the heel up through the ankle. The other is·to lift the heel with a slight spring, at the same time drawing the toes slightly under. Both ways are useful.

We rise up, rolling through the instep, when we relevé from a straight-knee position; and we spring up, drawing the toes under the instep, when we relevé from a demi-plié.

Generally, the rising from a straight knee is used for extremely quick and brilliant passages such as are found in some of the old classical ballets.

It is wise for beginners to start their practice with these rising relevés, working with straight knees throughout and taking them very slowly and carefully in very exact positions.

In coming down from the pointes always roll down the instep passing through the demi-pointe before the heel touches the floor. This is most important, for it is this control through the insteps that makes your movements light and soft.

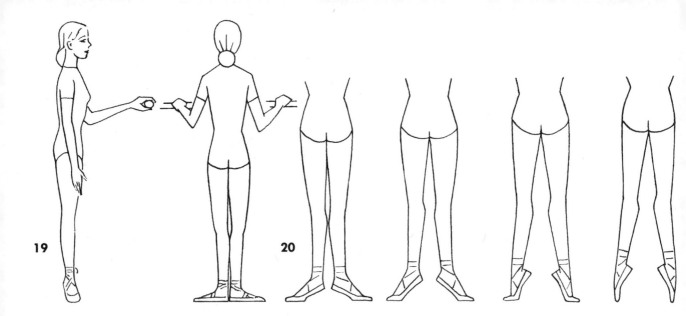

RELEVÉS FROM STRAIGHT-KNEE POSITIONS

19. Correct stance. Stand in First Position with perfect posture, correctly placed and well centered, with the weight of the body over the toes. The heels are held firmly to the floor, but they do not bear the weight of the body. Chin up, look straight out! Try not to lean on the barre as you *relevé* but rise up through the strength of your insteps, thighs, and back.

20. Rise to the quarter pointes, the demi-pointes, the three-quarter pointes, the full pointes, slowly, pulling up strongly through the knees and thighs and tightening the buttocks. Do not move the feet or permit the heels to twist back. Press the heels forward and do not sickle in nor out on the ankles. Roll down slowly, exactly as you rose, coming down gently through each level of the feet.

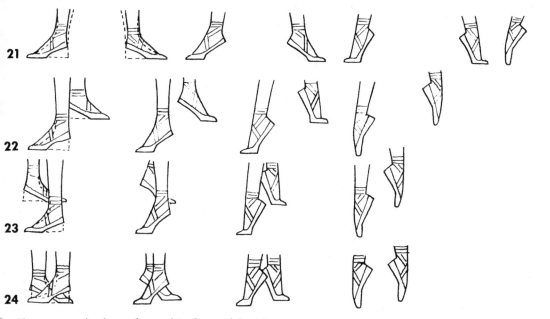

21. The same *relevés* performed in Second Position.

22. The same *relevés* performed in Open Fourth Position (Fourth Position out of First Position).

23. The same *relevés* performed in Crossed Fourth Position (Fourth Position out of Fifth Position).

24. The same *relevés* performed in Fifth Position.

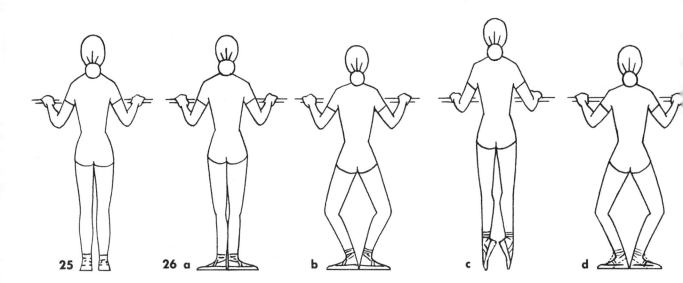

25   **26 a**   **b**   **c**   **d**

RELEVÉS FROM DEMI-PLIÉ

25. Face the barre and hold it firmly with both hands. Be sure that your posture is good and your placement correct. Remember that your feet are connected to your back through ligaments and muscles, so if you don't keep your back straight and strong, it will affect your footwork.

26. a. Stand in First Position

b. *demi-plié*, pressing both heels firmly into the flo

c. spring up, pushing strongly from the heels a drawing the toes slightly under the insteps so th you are in First Position on pointes with the to directly under the heels

d. slide the toes outward as you lower the hee gently but firmly to the floor into a *demi-plié*, wo through the *demi-pointe*, keep the heels forwar

. The same *relevé* in Second Position.

. The same *relevé* in Open Fourth Position.

. The same *relevé* in Crossed Fourth Position.

30. The same *relevé* in Fifth Position. Cross the feet so that they look like one foot. This is also called "*soussus*" and may be taken in place or traveling to the front, back, or side.

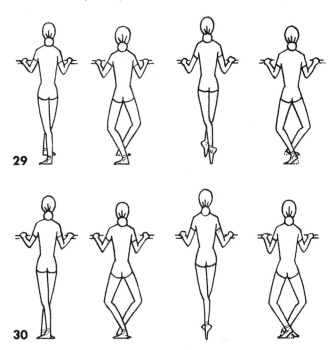

29

30

31. Don't lean on the barre. It takes the body out of its proper placement and balance.

32. Don't pull yourself up by pushing down on your arms. This is a good exercise for students of boxing, not ballet!

33. Don't push your stomach forward to achieve the position on pointes.

34. Don't let your heels twist back as you relevé.

35. Don't roll in on the arches or permit your knees to fall forward as you lower your heels.

36. Be sure to push the heels firmly into the floor each time you plié; don't let them pop up.

37. Don't let your back weaken.

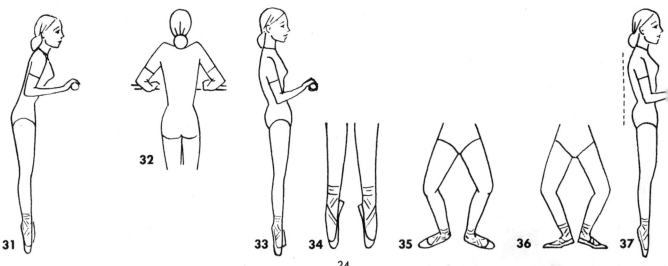

31 32 33 34 35 36 37

ÉCHAPPÉ ON POINTES

s in all of the steps described in this book the beginner
would perform this step first at the barre, and later,
when perfect control is gained, it may be practiced in the
center without the aid of the barre.

Échappés may be performed in Second Position or
Fourth Position. They may be taken *en face*, *en croisé*,
en effacé, or *en épaulé* and with or without changing of
the feet in Fifth Position.

ÉCHAPPÉ À LA SECONDE WITHOUT CHANGE OF FEET

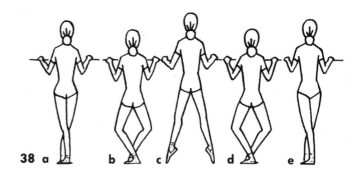

38 a   b   c   d   e

3. a. Ready to begin. Stand in Fifth Position with the
right foot front, facing the barre and holding it with
both hands, head erect, look straight out

b. *demi-plié* in this position (heels down, knees back,
body straight!). Count, "And . . ."

c. spring out to Second Position on pointes, pushing
off strongly with the heels. (Pull up the knees, tighten
the buttocks, lift up out of the hips, take a good,
wide Second Position.) Count, "One . . ."

d. return the feet to Fifth Position, *fondu*, right foot
front (both knees well opened out over the toes,
back straight and strong). Count, "And . . ." From
this *plié* you are ready to perform the next *échappé*

e. When you have finished a series of *échappés*,
such as eight or sixteen, finish nicely by straightening the knees.

Repeat the *échappé* with the left foot front. The
same *échappé* may also be performed changing the
feet each time they close to Fifth Position so that the
right foot alternately closes back and front.

39 a   b   c   d   e   f

ÉCHAPPÉ EN CROISÉ AND ÉCHAPPÉ CHANGÉ

Here is an example of the échappé to Fourth Position, in this case performed en croisé, followed by an échappé changé to Second Position.

39. a. Ready to begin: Stand in Fifth Position with the right foot front, facing en croisé, arms in Fifth Position Low, head inclined to the right

b. demi-plié in this position. Count, "And . . ."

c. spring out to Fourth Position on pointes, at the same time raise the arms through Fifth Position Front to Third Position High with the left arm up, incline the body slightly to the right. Count, "One . . ."

d. return the feet to Fifth Position, fondu, with right foot front, and at the same time lower the arm, in front of the face, to Fourth Position From Count, "And . . ."

e. spring out to Second Position on pointes, fac directly en face, and at the same time open the arm to Second Position. Count, "Two . . ."

f. close the feet to Fifth Position, fondu, with the foot front, and at the same time turn the body croisé and lower the arms to Fifth Position Lo Count, "And." Repeat the entire step to the ot side.

0. Don't keep the weight of the body over the back foot in Fourth Position, equalize the weight over both feet.

1. Don't permit the front leg to turn inward in the *échappé* in Fourth Position.

2. Don't mince the step by opening to a tiny Second Position.

3. Don't throw the feet so far apart that the position has no form.

40 **41** **42** **43**

RELEVÉ, FROM TWO FEET TO ONE FOOT

These *relevés* are sometimes called *relevé devant* and *relevé derrière,* sometimes *sissonne simple.* Terminology differs according to the Italian, French, and Russian schools. When the raised foot is transferred from the front to the back or from the back to the front, these *relevés* are called *relevé passé* or *sissonne passé le jambe.*

44. Stand in Fifth Position, right foot front, facing the barre and holding it with both hands. Have the body well centered, a good lift in the ribs, shoulders down, head erect, look straight out.

RELEVÉ DEVANT

45. a. *demi-plié.* Count, "And . . ."

b. spring up onto the left pointe and at the sar time raise the right foot to the *cou de pied deva* (or to the front of the left knee, in more advance work). Count, "One . . ."

c. close the right foot into Fifth Position, *fondu,* front of the left foot. Count, "And."

44

45a

b

c

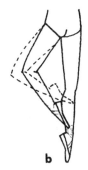

a   b   c   47 a   b   c

LEVÉ DERRIÈRE

. a. *demi-plié*. Count, "And . . ."

b. spring up onto the right pointe and at the same
time raise the left foot to the *cou de pied derrière*
(or behind the right knee, in more advanced work).
Count, "One . . ."

c. close the left foot into Fifth Position, *fondu*, behind the right foot. Count, "And."

RELEVÉ PASSÉ EN ARRIÈRE

47. a. *demi-plié*. Count, "And . . ."

b. spring up onto the left pointe and at the same
time raise the right foot to the front of the left knee.
Count, "One . . ."

c. close the right foot into Fifth Position, *fondu*, behind the left foot. Count, "And."

48. a. *demi-plié*. Count, "And . . ."

b. spring up onto the right pointe and at the same time raise the left foot to the back of the right knee. Count, "One . . ."

c. close the left foot into Fifth Position, *fondu,* in front of the right foot. Count, "And."

Repeat these *relevés* with the left foot front.

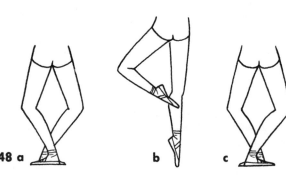

48 a   b   c

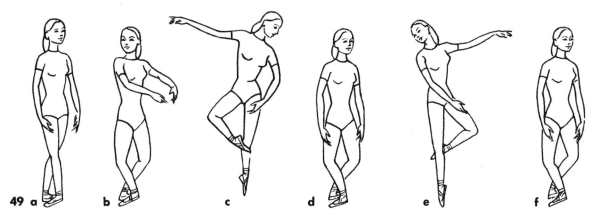

49 a   **b**   **c**   **d**   **e**   **f**

ELEVÉ DEVANT AND DERRIÈRE WITH AN EXAMPLE OF PORT DE BRAS AND BODY MOVEMENT

9. a. Ready to begin. Stand in Fifth Position, right foot front, facing *en croisé* (lower left corner of the room), arms in Fifth Position Low

   b. *demi-plié*. Count, "And . . ."

   c. spring up onto the left pointe, raising the right foot to the front of the left knee, incline the body and the head to the left and open the arms to Third Position Low, left arm front. Count, "One . . ."

   d. close the right foot into Fifth Position, *fondu*, in front of the left foot; at the same time straighten the body and return the arms to Fifth Position Low. Count, "And . . ."

   e. spring up onto the right pointe, raising the left foot to the back of the right knee, incline the body and the head to the right and open the arms to Third Position Low, right arm front. Count, "Two . . ."

   f. close the left foot into Fifth Position, *fondu*, behind the right foot; at the same time straighten the body and return the arms to Fifth Position Low. Count, "And."

Repeat this exercise several times with the right foot front, then repeat with the left foot front.

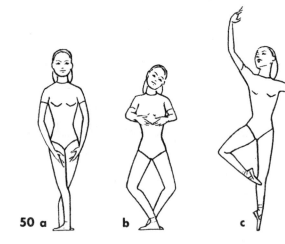

50 a   **b**   **c**   **d**

RELEVÉ PASSÉ EN ARRIÈRE WITH PORT DE BRAS

50. a. Ready to begin. Stand in Fifth Position, right foot front, facing *en face*, well centered, well lifted, arms in Fifth Position Low, head erect, look straight out

b. *demi-plié*, raise the arms to Fifth Position Front, incline the head to the left. Count, "And . . ."

c. spring up onto the left pointe, raising the right foot to the front of the left knee, open the arms to Third Position High with the right arm up, incline the body and the head to the left, look under the right

arm. Count, "One . . ."

d. close the right foot into Fifth Position, *fondu*, behind the left foot, open the arms outward and lower both of them to Fifth Position Low, incline the head to the right. Count, "And."

These *relevés* may be done in succession, alternating right foot and left foot. The arms must pass through Fifth Position Front each time before opening to Third Position High in order to give form to the movement.

32

RELEVÉ PASSÉ EN AVANT WITH PORT DE BRAS

a. Ready to begin

b. *demi-plié*. Count, "And . . ."

c. spring up onto the right foot, raising the left foot to the back of the right knee, raise the arms to Fourth Position Front with the left arm across the body, incline the body to the left knee, turn the head to the left, look at the left knee. Count, "One . . ."

d. close the left foot into Fifth Position, *fondu*, in front of the right foot, open the left hand out toward the lower left corner of the room. Count, "And."

In performing these *relevés* in succession the arms do not pass through Fifth Position Front but merely open and close as they alternate. There are, of course, other *ports de bras* that may be used in the *relevés passés*. Those illustrated here are examples of such movement.

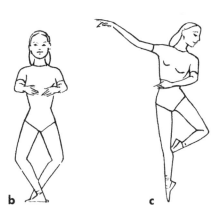

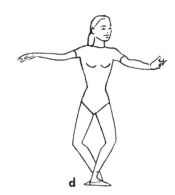

1 a   b   c   d

GLISSADE, ON POINTES

This step may be performed forward, backward, and sideward. It may be performed with a simple *dégagé* of the working foot or with a small *développé*. It may be done with or without changing the feet in closing to Fifth Position. The *glissade* illustrated here is with a change of feet.

GLISSADE CHANGÉE

52. a. Ready to begin. Stand in Fifth Position, right foot front, face the barre, hold it with both hands

b. slide the right foot out to a strong point in Second Position with a very straight knee, at the same time bend the left knee in a good *demi-plié*. Count, "And . . ."

c. step over onto the right pointe, taking the weight of the body over with you, pull both knees up tight. Count, "And . . ."

d. close the left foot, immediately, to Fifth Position on pointes, bringing it in front of the right, be sure to cross the feet well and pull both knees up tight. Count, "One . . ."

e. roll down the insteps, lowering both heels, gently but firmly, into a *demi-plié* in Fifth Position. Count,

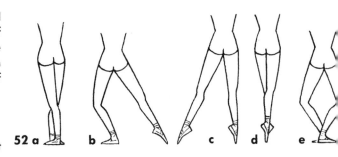

52 a   b   c   d   e

"And." If another *glissade* follows immediately, continue the "And" count into the sliding movement the leg to Second Position.

GLISSADE CHANGÉE
(with a small *développé*)

53. a. Ready. Stand in Fifth Position, left foot front, facing *en face*, left shoulder slightly front, head turned slightly to the left, eyes looking to the lower left corner of the room, arms in Fifth Position Low

b. *demi-plié* on the right leg, raising the left foot the *cou de pied devant*. Count, "And . . ."

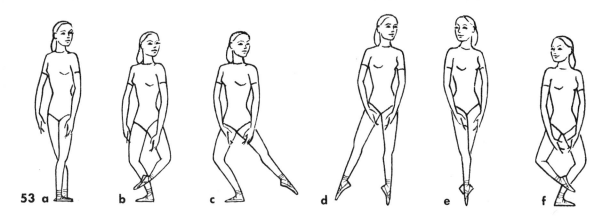

53 a   **b**   **c**   **d**   **e**   **f**

c. extend the left foot, straightening the knee in a low *développé;* this is part of the above "And . . ." count

d. step over onto the left pointe, taking the weight of the body with you, pull the knees up tight. Count, "A . . ."

e. close the right foot, immediately, to Fifth Position on pointes, in front of the left foot, bring the right shoulder slightly forward and turn the head slightly to the right, look to the lower right corner of the room, cross the feet well, and pull both knees up tight. Count, "One . . ."

f. roll down the instep of the left foot, gently lower-

ing the heel to the floor in *fondu;* at the same time raise the right foot to the *cou de pied devant.* Count, "And."

Remember that the manner in which you come down from the full-pointe position to the *pied à terre,* or whole foot on the ground, is most important. You should *always* roll down through the *demi-pointe,* never jump from the full pointe to the flat. This is what makes all the difference between light, airy, soft movement and hard, jerky movement.

Repeat the *glissade* with the left foot front. Repeat the *glissade* without changing the feet, both *derrière* and *devant.*

54 a   **b**   **c**   **d**

PIQUÉ

There are two ways of rising to a full-pointe position from the *pied à terre* position, where the whole foot rests on the floor.

One is the *relevé*, which has already been described, and the other is the *piqué*, or, as it is sometimes called, the *posé*. Again, the difference in terminology is that between the French and Italian schools. To *piqué* or *posé* means to step directly on to the full-pointe (or demi-pointe) position of the working foot and to raise the other foot into the air in any desired position such as *cou de pied, arabesque, attitude,* etc. *Piqués* may be performed to the front, to the back, to the side; they may be taken reaching out with the foot extended and the knee stretched, with or without a *développé,* or they may be taken close to the supporting foot, stepping with a bent knee and straightening it at the instant of stepping.

PIQUÉ EN ARRIÈRE, COUPÉ DESSUS

54. a. Stand in Fifth Position, right foot front, facing th
barre and holding it with both hands

b. *demi-plié* on the right leg, raising the left foot t
the *cou de pied derrière.* Count, "And . . ."

c. step directly onto the full pointe of the left foo
just behind the right foot, straightening the left kne
immediately as you step; at the same time raise th
right foot to the *cou de pied devant* (or to the knee
Count, "One . . ."

d. fall onto the right foot in a *coupé dessus*—that i
replace the left foot with the right, bending the kne

36

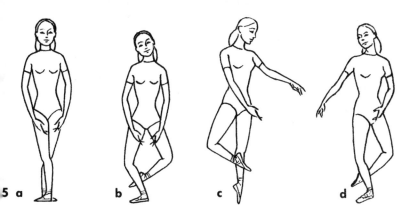

5 a　　　　b　　　　c　　　　d

in *fondu*, and at the same time raise the left foot to the *cou de pied derrière*. Count, "And."

Repeat the *piqué* with the left foot front.

The head plays an important part in all balletic movement. Here is the *piqué en arrière* and the *coupé dessus* performed with the movements of the head and arms:

a. Ready to begin. Stand in Fifth Position, right foot front, facing *en face*, head erect, arms in Fifth Position Low

b. *demi-plié* on the right leg and, as you raise the left foot to the *cou de pied derrière* position, incline the head to the right. Count, "And . . ."

c. *piqué en arrière*, at the same time open the arms to Third Position Low, with the right arm in front of the body, and incline the head to the left. Count, "One . . ."

d. *coupé dessus;* fall onto the right foot directly over the left foot, at the same time move the arms to the right into Third Position Low with the left arm in front and incline the head to the right. Count, "And." Take care that in the *coupé* you do not put the whole foot down flat but make the *fondu* movement of rolling down the instep as you *plié*.

Repeat the *piqué* with the left foot front.

The *piqué en arrière* may also be performed with an extended leg:

56. a. Ready. Stand in Fifth Position, right foot front, facing *en effacé* (lower right corner of the room), arms in Fifth Position Low

   b. *demi-plié* on the right leg, extending the left to *effacé derrière*, open the arms to the *demi-seconde* position. Count, "And . . ."

   c. step backward onto the full pointe of the left foot, stepping as far back as you can reach and taking the weight of the body with you as you ste[p] at the same time raise the right foot to the front [of] the left knee and carry the arms to Fourth Positi[on] Front. This may be done with either arm crosse[d] over the body. If the right arm is crossed over, le[an] the body forward slightly over the right knee (illu[s]trated), if the left arm is crossed over, lean the bod[y] and incline the head to the left. Count, "One . . [."]

   d. *coupé dessus*, extending the left leg once aga[in] to *effacé derrière*. Count, "And."

   Repeat the *piqué* with the left foot front.

56 a   **b**   **c**   **d**

   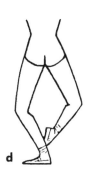 

7 a   b   c   d   58

QUÉ EN AVANT, COUPÉ DESSOUS

7. a. Stand in Fifth Position, right foot front, facing the barre, hold it with both hands

b. *demi-plié* on the left leg, raising the right foot to the *cou de pied devant*. Count, "And . . ."

c. step directly onto the pointe of the right foot just in front of the left foot, at the same time raise the left foot to the *cou de pied derrière* (or in back of the knee). Count, "One . . ."

d. *coupé dessous;* that is, fall onto the left foot, in *fondu*, under the right root, and at the same time raise the right foot to the *cou de pied devant*. Count, "And."

Repeat the *piqué* with the left foot front.

To perform the *piqué en avant* and *coupé dessous* in this manner with the head and arm movements, just reverse the action in Figure 55.

DON'T DO THIS!

58. Don't ever permit the supporting knee to be slack when standing on pointe. Always pull it up as tightly as possible. If the *piqué* is taken from a bent knee, straighten it at once as the weight is transferred. If the *piqué* is taken from an extended position, be sure that the knee is taut throughout.

The *piqué en avant* may also be taken with an extended leg:

59. a. Ready to begin. Stand in Fifth Position, left foot front, facing *en effacé*, head erect, arms in Fifth Position Low

    b. *demi-plié* on the right leg and *dégagé* the left leg to *effacé devant*, raise the arms to Fifth Position Front and incline the body and head to the right. Count, "And . . ."

    c. *piqué en avant;* that is, step directly onto the left pointe taking the weight of the body with you, and immediately raise the right foot to the *cou de pie derrière* (or back of the knee), at the same time rai the arms to Third Position High with the left arm hi and look under the arm. Count, "One . . ."

    d. *Coupé dessous,* that is fall on the right foot, fondu, directly under the left foot, cutting the left o to *effacé devant.* Count, "And."

Repeat the *piqué* with the right foot front.

This *piqué* may, of course, be performed with differe *ports de bras.* It may also be performed *en croisé* or face.

59 a   b   c   d

a b c d

UÉ EN ARABESQUE OUVERTE

a. Ready to begin. Stand in Fifth Position, left foot front, facing *en effacé* (lower left corner of the room), arms in Fifth Position Low, head inclined to right, look out

b. *demi-plié* on the right leg, raise the left foot to the *cou de pied devant*. Count, "And . . ."

c. extend the left foot in a small *développé*, straightening the left knee, and raise the arms to Fifth Position Front. Count, "A . . ."

d. *piqué en avant* into *arabesque*, stepping out as far as the toe can reach and carrying the weight of the body over with you, at the same time open the arms to *arabesque ouverte* (First Arabesque) and straighten the head, looking out over the top of the left hand. Count, "One."

Repeat the *piqué en arabesque* with the right foot.
Note carefully the difference between *piqué* and *relevé*.

41

PAS DE BOURRÉE PIQUÉ

When a *pas de bourrée* is said to be "*piqué*," this means that the movement is staccato, quick. As *piqué* means "pricked" or a pricking action, this literally means that the dancer pricks the floor with the sharp, quick, thrusting movements of the legs and feet.

This *pas de bourrée* may be taken *derrière*, *devant*, *dessous*, and *dessus*. The *pas de bourrée dessous* and *dessus* are often referred to as *pas de bourrée changé* because the feet change during the action of the step.

Described here is a *pas de bourrée changé—pas de bourrée piqué, dessous*.

61. a. Ready to begin. Stand in Fifth Position, right f front, facing the barre and holding it with both ha

b. *demi-plié* on the right leg, raising the left foo the *cou de pied derrière*. Count, "And . . ."

c. *piqué en arrière*, raising the right foot to the s of the left knee. Count, "One . . ."

d. without coming off pointe on the left foot, *pi* onto the right pointe, taking a step to the right s and raising the left foot to the side of the right kn Count, "And . . ."

e. without coming off pointe on the right foot, lo the left foot into Fifth Position on pointes in front the right. Count, "Two . . ."

f. *fondu* on the left leg; that is, roll down the ins through the *demi-pointe* into a good *demi-plié* the left heel on the floor; at the same time raise right foot to the *cou de pied derrière*. Co "And."

The action of raising the knees as you *piqué* sho be very sharp and the *piqué* should be marked strong.

Repeat the *pas de bourrée piqué* to the other side

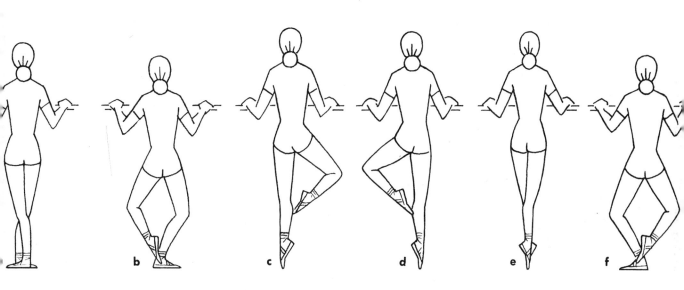

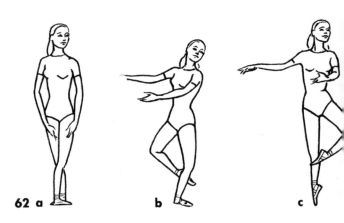

62 a   **b**   **c**

The *pas de bourrée* may be performed with many different *ports de bras*. Illustrated is a simple *port de bras* using the *épaulement*. Though the movements of the feet are sharp and staccato, the movements of the arms should not be jerky but should flow.

62. a. Ready to begin. Stand in Fifth Position with the left foot front, facing *en face*, left shoulder slightly front, arms in Fifth Position Low, head erect and slightly turned to the left

b. *demi-plié* on the left leg, at the same time r[...] the right foot to the *cou de pied derrière* and [...] arms to Fourth Position Front, bringing the left [...] across the body and inclining the body to the l[...] Count, "And . . ."

c. *piqué en arrière*, straightening the body and r[...] ing the left foot sharply to the side of the right kn[...] Count, "One . . ."

44

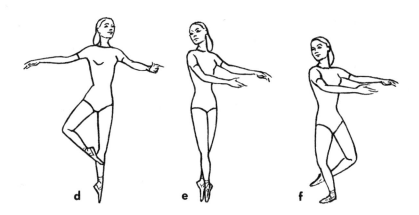

d.   e.   f.

d. without coming off the right pointe *piqué* onto the left pointe, taking a step to the left side and raising the right foot sharply to the side of the left knee; at the same time open the left arm out a little. Count, "And . . ."

e. without coming off pointe on the left foot close the right foot sharply into Fifth Position on pointes in front of the left, bring the right shoulder front and the right arm across the body as the left opens to second so that the arms are in Fourth Position Front with the right arm across, turn the head slightly to the right, holding it proudly erect, Count, "Two . . ."

f. *fondu* on the right leg, raising the left foot to the *cou de pied derrière* and inclining the body to the right. Count, "And."

The shoulder position and the head position should be well defined each time the *pas de bourrée* is repeated.

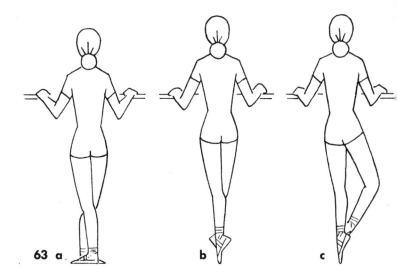

63 a   **b**   **c**

PAS DE BOURRÉE COURU, EN CINQUIÈME

This is a running *pas de bourrée* in Fifth Position, which may be performed traveling forward, backward, or sideward, in place, or turning in place.

While it appears simple, this is actually a very difficult step to master, owing to the flexion of the knees and the necessity for taking very tiny steps at a very rapid speed to give the impression of skimming smoothly over the surface of the floor or stage.

Since the action of the knees is difficult to master, the proper study of this step begins at the barre, performing the *bourrées* in place, concentrating on the correct move-

ment of the knees.

The following exercise, composed of tiny *piqués*, is good preliminary exercise to establish the correct feelin for the knee action.

63. a. Ready to begin. Stand in Fifth Position, right foc front, facing the barre and holding it with both hand

    b. *soussus*

    c. bend the right knee slightly, raising it an inch o the floor. Count, "And . . ."

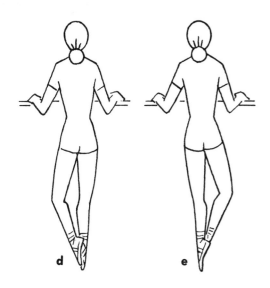

d. step on the pointe of the right foot in front of and close to the left foot, simultaneously bending the left knee and raising the left foot an inch off the floor. As you step on the pointe of the foot, pull up tightly on the supporting knee until it is completely straight. Count, "One . . ."

e. step on the pointe of the left foot behind and close to the right foot, simultaneously bending the right knee and raising the right foot an inch off the floor. As you step on the pointe, pull up tightly on

the supporting knee until it is completely straight. Count, "Two . . ." Continue, in this manner, to take these tiny *piqués*, being careful to keep the legs well turned out from the hips, the heels forward, and the feet well crossed in Fifth Position each time the foot is placed down.

Repeat this exercise with the left foot front.

This flexing and straightening action of the knees is what makes the smooth floating effect of the *pas de bourrée couru.*

When the action of the knees is well understood and easily performed, the next stage in the study of this *pas de bourrée* may be undertaken. This is to *bourrée* rapidly in place, flexing and straightening the knees and vibrating the feet from the ankles without taking them off the floor.

In traveling this action of the knees and feet must be preserved. Many students make the mistake of keeping their knees stiff in attempting the *bourrée*, others "sit" in the knees, giving them an ugly, bent appearance and the step a comical look.

The steps of the *pas de bourrée couru* MUST be tiny. The dancer travels by the speed of the feet rather than the size of the steps. The knees and feet must be kept close together at all times; in fact, the front foot is pushed along by the back foot. The legs must remain well turned out, the heels well forward, and the feet well crossed so that at all times the back foot is seen as well as the front foot. The arms may be used in any given manner.

Example of *port de bras* in *pas de bourrée couru*:

64. a. Stand on the right foot in a *demi-plié* with the left foot pointed to *croisé devant*, the body bent forward, head to the knee and inclined to the right, arms stretched forward and hands crossed at the wrists, left hand over right

b. *relevé*, drawing the extended foot into Fifth Position on pointes

4 a   **b**   **c**   **d**   **e**   **f**   **g**

c. travel to the left side with tiny *bourrée* steps, pass the arms through Fifth Position Front

d. continue to travel to the left with tiny steps, flexing and straightening the knees, pass the arms to Third Position High with the left arm up

e. continue to *bourrée* to the left and bring the right arm up to meet the left arm in Fifth Position High

f. step to the left with the left foot (off pointe) and pass the right foot to the *cou de pied*

g. take the right foot forward to *croisé devant*, sink into a good *demi-plié* on the left leg, at the same time bend the body forward, taking the head to the knee and inclining it to the left, stretch the arms forward, crossing the hands at the wrist with the right hand over the left.

Repeat the *pas de bourrée couru* to the other side.

ASSEMBLÉ SOUTENU, ON POINTES

DESSUS

65. a. Ready to begin. Stand in Fifth Position, left foot front, facing the barre, hold it with both hands. Head erect, body well centered and correctly placed.

b. slide the right foot out to a strong point in Second Position as the left leg bends in a good demi-plié. Count, "And . . ."

c. spring into Fifth Position on pointes, pushing force-fully off the left heel and drawing the right foot into position in front of the left. Count, "One . . ."

d. lower yourself gently to the demi-plié, passing through the demi-pointes.

Repeat this step with the right foot front.

To perform the assemblé soutenu dessous, reverse the action. Slide the front foot out to Second Position and close it behind in Fifth Position.

65 a   b   c   d

66 a   **b**   **c**   **d**   **e**

ASSEMBLÉ SOUTENU WITH AN EXAMPLE OF PORT DE BRAS DESSUS

66. a. Ready to begin. Stand in Fifth Position, left foot front, facing *en face*, arms in Fifth Position Low, head erect

b. as the right foot slides to Second Position, *fondu*, open the arms to *demi-seconde* position, incline the body to the right, look to the right foot. Count, "And . . ."

c. on the spring into Fifth Position, right foot front, carry the right arm across the body to the left side and raise both arms *a deux bras*, looking up to the top of the left hand, which is slightly higher than the right. Count, "One . . ."

d. lower into Fifth Position, *fondu*, and continue to slide the left foot out to the point in Second Position, open the arms to *demi-seconde* position, incline the body to the left, look to the left foot. Count, "And . . ."

e. spring again into Fifth Position on pointes, this time drawing the left foot into position in front of the right, carry the left arm across the body to the right side and raise both arms a *deux bras*, looking up to the top of the right hand, which is slightly higher than the right. Count, "Two."

DESSOUS

67. a. Ready to begin. Stand in Fifth Position, left foot front, facing *en face*, arms in Fifth Position Low, head erect

b. as the left foot slides out to Second Position, *fondu*, open the arms to *demi-seconde* position, incline the body to the right and the head to the right shoulder. Count, "And . . ."

c. on the spring into Fifth Position on pointes, draw the left foot into position behind the right, carry the left arm across the body to the right, raising both

arms *a deux bras*, look to the top of the right hand Count, "One . . ."

d. lower into Fifth Position, *fondu*, and continue to slide the right foot out to the point in Second Position, open the arms to *demi-seconde* position, incline the body to the left, and the head to the left shoulder. Count, "And . . ."

e. spring into Fifth Position on pointes, drawing the right foot into position behind the left, carry the right arm across the body to the left side, raising both arms *a deux bras*, look to the top of the left hand. Count, "Two."

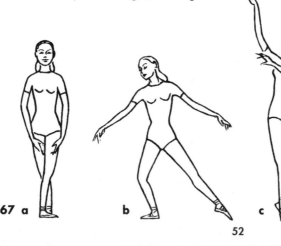

67 a   b   c   d   e

:OUPÉ SUR LA POINTE, FOUETTÉ RACCOURCI

68. a. Ready to begin. Stand in Fifth Position, right foot front, well centered, correctly placed, head erect, look straight out, arms in Fifth Position Low

b. *demi-plié* on the right leg, raising the left foot to the *cou de pied derrière* and the arms to Fifth Position Front, incline the head to the right. Count, "And . . ."

c. *piqué en arrière* on the left pointe (page 36), throwing the right leg to Second Position *en l'air*, *à la demi-hauteur* (45° angle) and opening both arms to *demi-seconde* position, head erect. Count, "One . . ."

d. lower into *demi-plié* on the left leg and at the same time whip the right foot behind the left leg, bending the right knee sharply without lowering the thigh, bring the arms into third position low and incline the body and head to the left. Count, "And . . ."

Repeat the *coupé* and *fouetté raccourci* with the other leg. The *port de bras* may also be taken with the arm in front corresponding to the raised leg and the body inclined to the raised knee at the finish of the *fouetté raccourci*.

69 a   b   c   d

BALLONNÉ, ON POINTE

69. a. Stand in Fifth Position, right foot front, facing the barre, back straight, head erect

   b. *demi-plié* on the left leg and raise the right foot to the *cou de pied devant*. Count, "And . . ."

   c. spring up to a *relevé* on the left foot and throw the right foot out in a strong *développé* movement to Second Position *en l'air, à la demi-hauteur*. Do not raise the thigh; the movement takes place from the knee joint. Count, "One . . ."

   d. roll down the instep of the left foot into a *demi plié* and bring the right foot back to the *cou de pied* position. Do not lower the thigh; the movement takes place from the knee joint. Count, "And."

   Repeat this step several times on the same foot. Re peat it with the other foot. The working leg may also be closed in back of the ankle or it may alternate front and back.

54

70 a   **b**   **c**   **d**

Ballonné on pointe may be performed in the center, in either *écarté* or *effacé* direction with the foot extending to Second Position or to Fourth Position, traveling diagonally across the stage. It is here illustrated in *effacé*.

70. a. Ready to begin. Stand in Fifth Position, left foot front, facing *en effacé* (lower left corner of room), arms in Fifth Position Low, head inclined to right, look straight out

b. *demi-plié* on the right leg, raising the left foot to the *cou de pied devant* and the arms to Fifth Position Front. Count, "And . . ."

c. spring up to a *relevé* on the right foot, traveling forward a little, throw the left foot out into a strong *développé* in Fourth Position *en l'air, à la demi-hauteur*, open the arms to Third Position High with the right arm high. Head is inclined to the raised arm. Count, "One . . ."

d. roll down the instep of the right foot into a *demi-plié* and bring the left foot back to the *cou de pied* position. The arms remain in Third Position High. Travel a little forward on the *plié*. Count, "And." Remember to keep the legs turned out from the hips, the heels forward, the back straight and strong, the working leg moving from the knee without raising and lowering the thigh.

These *ballonnés* may be performed in a series of 4, 8, 16, or 32 on the same foot.

71 a   **b**   **c**   **d**

SISSONNE, ON POINTE

Sissonnes may be taken on pointe in any desired pose and in various directions of the body. The *sissonne* may be opened with a *développé* or without. It may travel to the front, to the back, or to the side.

SISSONNE EN ARABESQUE

71. a. Ready to begin. Stand in Fifth Position, left foot front, facing *en croisé* (lower right corner of room), head inclined to the right, arms in Fifth Position Low

b. *demi-plié*. Push the heels firmly into the floor Count, "And . . ."

c. spring up and out to *arabesque ouverte* (First Arabesque) on the left pointe, turning the body to face the left wall and traveling as much as possible Count, "One . . ."

d. close the right foot into Fifth Position, *fondu*, in front of the left foot, facing *en croisé* (lower left corner), head inclined to the left and arms lowered to Fifth Position Low. Count, "And."

Repeat the *sissonne* on the other foot.

RELEVÉS ON ONE FOOT

This difficult step requires a great deal of strength in the back, the thighs, and the insteps. It is wise to practice these relevés diligently at the barre, not attempting to perform them in the center, until such time as the necessary strength can be commanded. Relevés on one foot may be performed in any given pose; they may be done in one place or traveling, facing in any of the body directions, or turning in place.

ELEVÉ EN ARABESQUE

2. a. Face the barre, hold it with both hands. Stand on the right foot, well turned out from the hip, with the left leg extended back in *arabesque à terre*, well turned out from the hip and having the foot correctly pointed on the edge of the big toe with the heel pressed down

b. *demi-plié*, hold the back strong. Count, "And . . ."

c. spring up into a *relevé* on the right foot, drawing the toes under the heel as you spring, pull the knees up tight, maintain the turn out of the legs, do not pull on the barre. Count, "One . . ."

d. lower, through the *demi-pointe*, into the *demi-plié* on the right leg. Maintain the strength of the back, do not permit the left leg to drop, keep a strong point in the left foot. Count, "And."

Repeat this *relevé* in a series of 4, 8, or 16 on the same foot. Repeat the series of *relevés* with the other foot.

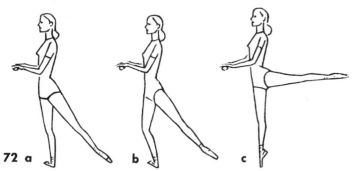

72 a b c   d

73. a. Ready to begin. Stand in Fifth Position, right foot front, facing *en croisé* (lower left corner), arms in Fifth Position Low.

b. *demi-plié* and *chassé* forward to Fourth Position Croisé, taking the weight of the body forward over the front knee, which remains bent as the back knee straightens, raise the arms to Fifth Position Front and incline the head to the left. Count, "And . . ."

c. spring up into a *relevé* in *attitude croisé* on the right pointe, pushing off both heels forcefully. Draw the toes under the body, arch the back, press the shoulders down and the left shoulder forward, cline the head to the right, pull the right knee tight, raise the left knee, bend it sharply at a rig angle, cross the left leg well over in the back. Cou "One . . ."

d. lower into a *demi-plié* on the right leg, maintai ing the good *attitude* position. Don't forget to r down the instep through the *demi-pointe*. Cou "And . . ."

e. repeat the *relevé* in *attitude croisé* on cou "Two."

Repeat this *relevé* in a series of 4, 8, or 16 on ea foot.

73 a   **b**   **c**   **d**   **e**

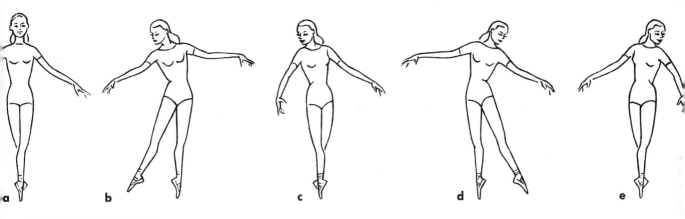

a   b   c   d   e

MBOÎTÉ SUR LES POINTES

his step is quite different from the *emboîté* that is *sauté*.
mboîté on pointes is a series of walking steps on the
ointes performed in Fifth Position.

'4. a. Ready to begin. Stand in Fifth Position, left foot
front, facing *en face*, arms in *demi-seconde*. *Demi-
plié* and *soussus*

b. keeping both knees pulled up tightly, *dégagé* the
right foot to a small Second Position, bend forward
slightly and look toward the right foot. Count,
"And . . ."

c. close the right foot into Fifth Position, on pointes,
in front of the left foot. Count, "One . . ."

d. *dégagé* the left foot to a small Second Position,
looking toward the left foot. Count, "And . . ."

e. close the left foot into Fifth Position, on pointes,
in front of the right foot. Count, "Two."

Continue to walk in this manner, advancing toward
the front of the room, and crossing the feet well
each time in Fifth Position. Keep the insteps well
pulled up at all times.

When the action is reversed and the feet close behind in Fifth Position each time, so that the dancer
recedes from the front of the stage to the back, this
step is called "*déboîté.*"

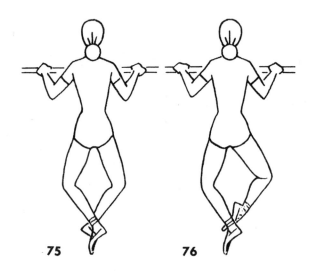

75   **76**

DEMI-PLIÉ, ON POINTES

In taking the *demi-plié* on pointes the dancer must hold the ankle very strong. The arch does not force over—on the contrary, the instep and ankle are tense and the heel is held firmly. Beginners will find this very difficult to do and should approach the study of this movement slowly and carefully, practicing it first on two feet in all the po-

sitions, later on one foot, when the instep is sufficiently strong to hold under this pressure.

75. *Demi-plié* in Fifth Position.

76. *Demi-plié* on one foot.
    This *demi-plié* may be practiced at the barre in many ways. An example is the *jeté piqué*.

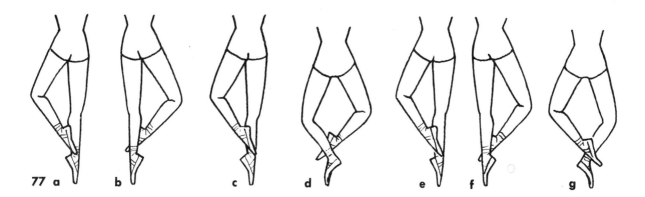

77 a   b   c   d   e   f   g

7. a. From Fifth Position with the right foot front, facing the barre and holding it with both hands, *demi-plié* and execute a *relevé derrière* (page 29). Count, "and . . ."

b. *jeté piqué* onto the left foot. That is, without coming down off pointe step onto the left foot directly under the right and raise the right foot to the *cou de pied devant*. Pull the left knee up tight, press the right knee well open. Count, "One . . ."

c. *jeté piqué* onto the right foot. That is, without coming down off pointe step onto the right foot directly over the left and raise the left foot to the *cou de pied derrière*. Pull the right knee up tight and press the left knee well open. Count, "And . . ."

d. *jeté piqué en fondu* onto the left foot. That is, bend the left knee in a *demi-plié* as you step on the left pointe. Press both knees well open. Count, "Two, and . . ."

e. *jeté piqué* onto the right foot. Count, "One . . ."

f. *jeté piqué* onto the left foot. Count, "And . . ."

g. *jeté piqué en fondu* onto the right foot, incline the head to the right. Count, "Two, and."

Continue to repeat this set of steps several times on the same side. Then repeat on the other side.

When the insteps are strong enough, this same exercise may be performed in the center without the aid of the barre.

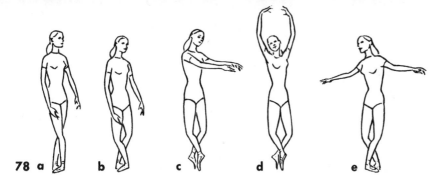

78 a   b   c   d   e

SAUTÉ SUR LES POINTES

Jumps on pointe are among the most difficult technical feats to perform and they should not be undertaken until the full strength of the feet, legs and, back has been developed. Much practice on the *demi-pliés* on pointe should precede the study of jumps on pointe. When you are able to hold the ankles and heels strongly in the *demi-pliés,* you are ready to begin the study of jumps on pointe.

Jumping on pointe may be performed on two feet, on one foot, or from foot to foot.

SAUTÉ SUR LES POINTES AND CHANGEMENT

78. a. Ready to begin. Stand in Fifth Position, right foot front, facing *en croisé* (lower left corner), arms in Fifth Position Low

b. *demi-plié,* incline the head to the left. Coun "And . . ."

c. jump up onto the pointes in Fifth Position, rigl foot front, raise the arms to Fifth Position From head remains inclined to the left. Count, "One . . .

d. jump again on the pointes without changing tl feet, raise the arms to Fifth Position High, look und the arms. Count, "And . . ."

e. *changement,* off pointes, finishing in a *demi-pl* in Fifth Position with the left foot front. As you jum turn the body to face the lower right corner, so th you are again facing *en croisé,* and open the arn outward to Second Position with the palms open, i cline the body and the head to the right. Coun "Two, And."

Repeat the entire step on the other side.

PAS DE CHEVAL

This step gets its name from the fact that it resembles the action of the horse as it paws the ground.

9. a. Ready to begin. Stand in Fourth Position on pointes, facing *en effacé* (lower left corner), with the left foot pointed front, the right knee bent in a *demi-plié*, arms in *demi-seconde*, body bent slightly forward, look toward the left foot

b. spring lightly upward off the right pointe and raise the left foot to the right knee. Count, "And . . ."

c. alight on the pointe of the left foot in *demi-plié* and raise the right foot to the left knee. Count, "A . . ."

d. without stopping the action of the right leg continue to develop it to Fourth Position *à la demi-hauteur*. This is part of the same count as c. (above)

e. continue the movement of the right foot until it points out on the floor. Count, "One."

Repeat the step with the other foot. Continue to repeat the step, alternating the feet and traveling diagonally downstage.

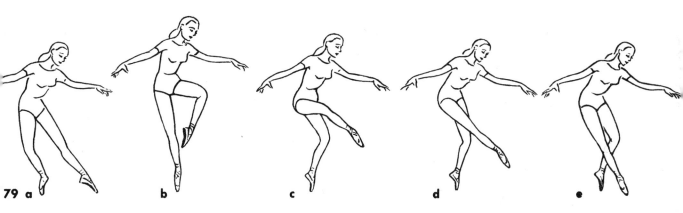

79 a　　　　**b**　　　　**c**　　　　**d**　　　　**e**

SAUTILLÉ SUR LA POINTE

Little hops on the pointe of one foot are often the high-light of the variations from classical repertoire. They may be performed in any given pose and also chang-ing from one pose to another. For example: the dancer may begin with a *relevé* in *attitude devant*. From this position she will hop lightly and rapidly on the sup-porting pointe, carrying the raised leg slowly aroun from *attitude devant* to *attitude effacé*, traveling backward the entire time. When she has reached th *attitude effacé* and the end of the sequence of hops she will sharply straighten both knees into a pose i *effacé derrière*, holding the balance on pointe a long as possible before closing the feet to Fift Position off pointe.

2353

64